Her Eyes on the S

Maria Mitchell, Astronomer

By Laurie Wallmark

Illustrated by Liz Wong

Night after night, Maria and her father climbed the stairs to her magical world — their rooftop observatory. On moonless nights, she loved sweeping the heavens with their telescope.

Who knew what she'd see? Stars and planets, of course.
Maybe a shooting star. Or even a comet.

In 1831, when Maria was twelve, she and her father observed a solar eclipse, when the moon crossed in front of the sun. The sky grew darker, and songbirds fell silent. Their surroundings grew unnaturally still.

The moon cast a shadow that passed over their small island of Nantucket. But this was no ordinary eclipse. It was a rare annular eclipse, where the moon was too far from Earth to completely block the sun. At totality, people in the right place would see the sun peek around the edges of the moon and glow like a ring of fire.

Maria desperately wanted to see that once-in-a-lifetime sight, but Nantucket was not in the path of totality. Before the eclipse reached its peak, the sun and the moon sank below the horizon. All she saw was a partial eclipse. Maria was determined to see so much more.

But she didn't want to just see objects in the sky, she wanted to understand them. As her father had taught her, Maria used sky charts and a chronometer, an extremely accurate timepiece, to make and record astronomical measurements.

When she was only thirteen, while her father was away, a whaling-ship captain asked for her help. He wanted her to use her knowledge of astronomical tools to determine how accurate his maritime chronometer was. To do this, Maria would need to take astronomical measurements and use math to give him the answer.

Sailors used these timepieces for celestial navigation — to steer by the stars. The captain needed to know exactly how slow or fast his chronometer ran. That way, he could make the proper correction to the time and determine his ship's accurate position. If he didn't, a ship might get lost at sea or even run aground.

This was Maria's first time checking a precision instrument by herself. Lives depended on her making sure the chronometer worked accurately. She had to get it right.

And she did!

Not only did the captain pay her, but Maria was on the path to becoming a professional astronomer.

At eighteen, determined to make her own way in the world, Maria took a job as a librarian, one of the few jobs open to women at the time. But she didn't give up on astronomy.

When the library was empty, Maria taught herself celestial mechanics, the science of how to calculate the motion of objects in the sky. The notebook she always carried overflowed with complex calculations that determined the exact positions and paths of astronomical bodies.

After work, she climbed back to the roof and her telescope. Night after night, season after season, Maria recorded the locations and movements of constellations, planets, and other celestial bodies.

In the winter, she often had to shovel a walkway through the rooftop snow. Her numb fingers struggled to adjust the telescope's mechanism. The frigid air froze the ink and she had to use a pencil to write notes. But that didn't stop Maria.

One October evening in 1847, Maria joined her parents at a dinner party they were hosting. She soon grew bored, because nobody was talking about astronomy. Eager to get back to her beloved night sky, Maria sneaked out to the rooftop.

Through the telescope, Maria saw a fuzzy white blur in an unexpected place. No matter how she adjusted her lens, she couldn't bring it into focus.

Could it be? Had she found a comet?

To prove this, Maria had to confirm the object moved through the night sky. Maybe it was only a nebula — a far-off cloud of gas and dust — that had already been discovered. She frowned. Maria had to find out.

Through her telescope, she spent hours measuring the cotton ball's distance to other astronomical objects. Had it moved? Maria sighed and laid down her notebook. She couldn't tell. Not enough time had passed.

The next day, Maria could hardly wait until nightfall. Would her little piece of fuzz still be there? Would it be in the same place?

She quickly found her cotton ball in the sky. Carefully, she measured its exact location.

Her observations showed that the object had shifted position slightly. She checked her measurements over and over again.

It *had* moved!

At age twenty-nine, Maria became the first American to discover a comet!

She ran to share the exciting news with her parents. Maria spent many hours calculating the orbit of what she called her "Comet of the Tenth Month," now known as Comet Mitchell 1847IV.

The King of Denmark had established a prize for the first person to discover a new telescopic comet — one invisible to the naked eye. To claim the award for Maria, her father wrote a letter to the director of the Harvard University Observatory. He included all of Maria's observations and calculations.

Because of bad weather, several days passed before his letter could leave Nantucket Island.

The contest rules required that the comet finding be reported to the British Astronomer Royal, but Maria and her father didn't know this. Would she lose the prize because they hadn't sent their letter to the right person?

Within days of Maria's sighting, three European astronomers also saw the comet. Each of them sent a letter to the Astronomer Royal, thinking they had seen it first. Would one of them win the prize?

Although Maria's information arrived later than theirs, news of "Miss Mitchell's Comet" quickly spread throughout Europe. Newspapers called her the "Lady Astronomer."

Since Maria's notes proved she had made the earliest observation of the comet, astronomers around the world declared she deserved the honor of being named its discoverer.

The Danish king agreed, and he awarded her the gold medal and prize money.

Two years later, Maria finally got a job as a professional astronomer. The United States Naval Observatory hired her to compute the daily position of Venus for its Nautical Almanac, one of the top jobs available for an astronomer.

Published yearly, the Almanac gave the accurate location of many stars and planets for each day of the coming year. Navigators needed this information to use celestial navigation. Even a tiny mistake in her computations might cause a ship to go astray and be shipwrecked.

These calculations were as important as fixing maritime chronometers had been, but on a much bigger, more complicated scale.

To calculate Venus's locations, Maria had to consider many factors: the sun's motion; the earth's daily rotation; the earth's revolution around the sun; and the elliptical orbit of Venus itself. These all changed from day to day. The work was challenging, but she loved it.

She received $300 (equal to about $10,000 today) for each annual volume of the Nautical Almanac. Maria was proud to be one of the few paid astronomers of the time. She was the first professional woman astronomer in America and one of the first women employed professionally by the government in any kind of job. For nineteen years, Maria calculated the daily position of Venus for the Almanac.

In 1865, the founders of a new women's school, Vassar College, offered Maria a job as a professor of astronomy, one of their first faculty members. She accepted, becoming the first female astronomy professor in the world.

Maria knew she was training the next generation of women astronomers. And she was determined there would be a next generation. She told her classes, "We are women working together." In 1906, three of her former female students were good enough to be included in the first list of Academic Men of Science. This was a major achievement for all women in science.

In 1885, Maria witnessed her last eclipse. Because Vassar was not in the path of totality of this rare annular eclipse, she missed the ring of fire once again. Instead she saw another powerful ring — a ring of women.

Surrounded by her students, Maria watched as the moon slowly but surely crept across the sun's surface. Increasing darkness and silence surrounded her and her team.

Fifty–four years after she and her father had first witnessed an eclipse together, Maria now shared this eclipse with a new generation of astronomers, young women aiming for the stars.

MARIA'S RULES OF ASTRONOMICAL OBSERVATION

Plan in advance for what you desire to see — good or bad. If you have clouds, you have at least gained by thinking it over.

Record — Write down all that you do see — good or bad — weak or strong. You need not publish it!

Be honest — Avoid the temptation to see what you expected to see. Do not try to make the eyes catch the objects, but let the objects catch the eye.

GLOSSARY

Astronomy: the branch of science which deals with objects in the sky, space, and the physical universe as a whole

Aurora: a natural light display in the Earth's sky, predominantly seen closer to the polar regions

Chronometer: a clock designed to keep accurate time in spite of motion or change in temperature, humidity, and air pressure

Celestial: having to do with the sky or outer space

Celestial navigation: steering by the stars; finding one's way by computing the angle between the horizon and celestial objects such as planets, the sun, and the stars

Comet: cosmic snowball of frozen gases, rock, and dust that orbits the sun

Heavens: having to do with outer space

Solar eclipse: when the moon passes in front of the sun and casts a shadow on the Earth

Maritime: having to do with the sea, especially commercial or military activity

Nautical Almanac: a publication that describes the position of selected celestial bodies so navigators can steer by the stars

Nebula: a far-off cloud of gas and dust that appears to be fixed in the sky

Observatory: a room or building that houses a telescope for the study of astronomical or other natural phenomena

Shooting star: a small, rapidly moving body of matter that burns up on entering the earth's atmosphere

TYPES OF SOLAR ECLIPSES

A *solar eclipse* occurs when the moon passes in front of the sun and casts a shadow on the Earth. For this to happen, the sun, moon, and Earth have to line up with the moon between the Earth and sun.

There are three types of solar eclipses: *total, partial,* and *annular:*

Total eclipse: The moon completely hides the bright light of the sun so only the faint solar corona can be seen.

Partial eclipse: The moon only partially hides the sun from view.

Annular eclipse: The moon and sun are in line with the Earth, but the moon appears smaller than the sun.